Sports for Supergirls

Sports in the Wild

Louise Spilsbury

Gareth Stevens
PUBLISHING

Please visit our website, **www.garethstevens.com**.
For a free color catalog of all our high-quality books,
call toll free 1-800-542-2595 or fax 1-877-542-2596.

Cataloging-in-Publication Data

Names: Spilsbury, Louise.
Title: Sports in the wild / Louise Spilsbury.
Description: New York : Gareth Stevens Publishing, 2020. | Series: Sports for supergirls
| Includes glossary and index.
Identifiers: ISBN 9781538242216 (pbk.) | ISBN 9781538241943 (library bound)
Subjects: LCSH: Outdoor recreation--Juvenile literature. | Extreme sports--Juvenile literature.
| Women athletes--Juvenile literature.
Classification: LCC GV191.62 S65 2020 | DDC 796.5--dc23

First Edition

Published in 2020 by
Gareth Stevens Publishing
111 East 14th Street, Suite 349
New York, NY 10003

Produced by Calcium
Editors: Sarah Eason and Jennifer Sanderson
Designers: Clare Webber and Jeni Child

Photo credits: Cover: Shutterstock: Pressmaster; Inside: Flickr: Scott Waraniak: pp. 35t; 37; Eric Wheeler:
p. 15; Positraction: Shelby Anderon: pp. 41t, 41b; Shutterstock: Nate Allred: p. 17b; Anatoliy_gleb: p. 9t; Alex
Brylov: p. 14; Ysbrand Cosijn: p. 17t; Deep Desert Photography: p. 6; Dm_Cherry: pp. 18, 45; DMartin09: p. 5t;
Greg Epperson: pp. 4, 13; Matteo Gabrieli: p. 31; Goodluz: p. 25; HeyPhoto: pp. 3, 40; Homydesign: p. 38; Jukkis:
p. 29; Vytautas Kielaitis: p. 39; Dudarev Mikhail: p. 5b; Antoni Murcia: p. 23b; Vitalii Nesterchuk: p. 12; Steve
Oehlenschlager: p. 19; Pedrosala: pp. 1, 7, 32; Mike Pellinni: p. 36; PHB.cz (Richard Semik): p. 24; Phonix_a
Pk.sarote: p. 43; Photobac: p. 10; Bob Pool: p. 9b; PRESSLAB: pp. 16, 21, 22; Ptnphoto: p. 8; Joshua Resnick:
p. 42; Salajean: p. 30; SaveJungle: p. 28; Sementer: p. 33; Studio 72: p. 34; Pavel Svoboda Photography: p. 26;
Aleksei Verhovski: p. 20; Brian Wolski: p. 27; Wwwarjag: p. 23t; Zhukovvvlad: p. 11; Z.o.y.a: p. 35b.

CPSIA compliance information: Batch #CS19GS:
For further information contact Gareth Stevens, New York, New York at 1-800-542-2595.

Contents

For a long time, sports in the wild were seen as too dangerous and extreme for girls and women to take part in. Not anymore... Today, women are strapping on their hiking boots, getting their gear, and heading out into the countryside for some wild adventures!

WILD SPORTS

Sports in the wild are sports and activities that people do in the great outdoors, up mountains, in forests, by rivers, or other remote wild places. There are many different kinds of sports that people do in the wild, from fishing and hunting to caving, climbing, and motocross. Thankfully, the idea that these fun sports are only for boys is as old-fashioned as black-and-white televisions. Why should girls and women not love hiking the hills, rafting in rivers, and scaling mountains?

Taking on the challenge of wild sports like rock climbing is exhilarating and exciting.

WHY GO WILD?

Sports in the wild are a great way for everyone to try a new challenge and to get some exercise outdoors in fresh air. For example, hiking is a great way to exercise the body and to keep fit. It strengthens the leg muscles as well as the heart and lungs. Pounding along on uneven trails and rocky paths also helps keep bones strong.

Walkers in the wild may need to watch out for animals like bears and venomous snakes.

THE FEEL-GOOD FACTOR

Getting outdoors and doing something exciting and physical makes people feel great. Fresh air and fun help people sleep longer and better, and that means they wake feeling refreshed. Being outdoors with friends and achieving something positive also gives people a feeling of exhilaration. While working out, it is easy for people to forget their everyday worries. The buzz participants get from outdoor sports stays with them for hours after hanging up their boots.

GIRL TALK

In the outdoors, there may be wild animals, so anyone heading for somewhere remote should check what wildlife lives there and what precautions they should take, if any. Meeting a bear or dangerous snake on a lonely trail is not anyone's idea of fun.

Women who tackle wild sports are able to see some of the most beautiful natural places in the world.

A Man's World?

Tackling steep mountains and deep canyons, and the threat of fierce storms or wild animals and other hazards, make wild sports challenging. Be advised: While sports in the wild may be for both women and men, they aren't for the fainthearted!

SAY HELLO TO HIKING

A hike is not a gentle stroll through town. It is a long, vigorous walk, usually on trails in the countryside, often over terrain that includes mountains, hills, and coastline. Hiking is easy for anyone to do, in that all people really need is a pair of walking boots and some weather-appropriate clothing to keep warm or from getting sunburned. Walking in the wild gives people the chance to experience some majestic scenery, but it can also be tiring and, on steep stretches of a hike, physically demanding.

Hiking takes effort, but hikers will be rewarded with great views and getting closer to nature.

Rappelling down the wall of a canyon is an exciting skill to try to master.

CRAZY FOR CANYONEERING

Some people hike to canyons for another form of wild sport: canyoneering. Canyoneering involves moving through canyon features such as crevices, rivers, and waterfalls in different ways. It combines rock climbing, hiking, and even the occasional swim. The way that most people get down into a canyon is by rappelling, which is sliding down the side of a steep vertical drop holding a rope.

WILD CAMPING

While hiking or heading to remote canyons, people often stay overnight in the wild. One of the great joys of camping is the chance to sleep under the stars in beautiful countryside. It is important for campers to check that they are not on private property and also for them to leave the spot as they found it when they move on. As well as a tent, campers need a sleeping bag and other basic essentials such as water, food, and warm, waterproof clothes for cooler nights.

GIRL TALK

One of the biggest dangers people face when canyoneering is a flash flood. A canyon can be flooded by a sudden storm that is happening miles away, so before it even rains in a canyon, people can find themselves in deep water. It is vital to check the weather report before any wild trip. If storms are forecast, canyoneers should call it off.

Going the Distance

Some girls take hiking to a whole new level. Instead of trekking a day or two in the hills, they set off on hikes that cover hundreds of miles. They often do this alone, with only the supplies they carry in their backpack to see them through.

GOT YOUR GEAR?

Getting lost is a common hazard on long-distance walks, so most hikers take a global positioning system (GPS) navigation device with them. A printed map and compass are good to have, too, in case the GPS or phone runs out of power. Other equipment required for hiking includes sturdy hiking boots, water, food, sunglasses, sunscreen, and rainproof clothing. Most people also carry a trekking pole, a flashlight, a first aid kit, a fire starter, and a knife. Gloves, insect repellent, and an emergency blanket may also be useful.

GIRL TALK

Hikers should remember that they are putting themselves in potentially scary situations in remote places, where rescue missions are difficult to carry out. They should always tell people where they intend to go and when they are planning to return. This way, someone will know where to start looking if something goes wrong.

A handheld GPS device is useful because it allows walkers to easily find their way.

ELIZABETH THOMAS —THE SNORKEL

Elizabeth Thomas has backpacked more than 15,000 miles (24,000 km) across the United States on 20 long-distance hikes. She got her trail name "Snorkel" after spending a cold night with her head inside her sleeping bag, until moisture in her breath made the sleeping bag soggy. A store worker joked that she needed a snorkel to breathe out of her sleeping bag, and the name Snorkel stuck.

Liz advises all girls who hike to make sure they take the right equipment with them, such as hiking poles.

STAY FOCUSED

Liz loves backpacking because she says it allows her to focus on what really matters. It clears the noise from life and provides a space where she can connect with nature, with others, and with herself. Her advice to anyone wanting to take a long-distance hiking challenge is to pack ultralight. Minimizing the weight in a backpack if trekking thousands of miles helps reduce damage to the body. To keep safe, she recommends learning wilderness skills and first aid. This advice has helped her finish the long-distance hikes of her dreams.

The motto for protecting the wild places where people hike and camp is: Leave nothing but footprints. Take nothing but photos. Kill nothing but time. Keep nothing but memories.

Chapter 2

Rock Climbing

Rock climbing is a great example of a wild sport in which women are being given the chance to do things that people normally would not expect of them. In the past, there were fewer women than men climbing on rocks. But today, there is a boom in rock climbing and many climbers are women.

Rock climbers get an adrenaline rush from completing a climb as well as a great full-body workout.

TIME TO GET TOUGH

Rock climbing is as much about mental strength as it is about physical strength. Sports coaches describe mental toughness as the ability to perform in difficult situations. When climbing steep cliffs, people inevitably meet challenges. Maybe the weather changes, their arms suddenly feel weak, or it is taking longer than they planned. At those moments, it is determination and focus that get a climber to the top, not just muscles.

LEADING A CLIMB

To help other climbers by securing a rope, a lead climber has to climb the cliff first. Lead climbing is a risky business. As a lead climber ascends, or goes up, a cliff, they fix bolts into the rock face. They then clip a rope, which trails to the ground below, into the bolts. The lead climber is harnessed to this rope, so if they fall they will not fall right to the bottom of the cliff, though the fall will be at least twice as long as the distance above the last bolt.

BOULDERING

Some female climbers push the limits of their sport by doing a type of rock climbing called bouldering. Bouldering is climbing up rock formations without the use of ropes or harnesses. Instead, climbers use shoes with extra grip and chalk on their hands to help them get a tight hold on steep rock walls, which are usually less than 20 feet (6 m) high.

GIRL TALK

While most boulderers and rock climbers love their sport best when they are clambering over rocks in the wild, artificial climbing walls allow them to train indoors. Indoor climbing is a great option for those who live in cities or far from rocky regions.

Bouldering is a tricky but exciting skill for rock climbers to learn.

Young Crushers

The best rock climbers are known as crushers because they can demolish a rock face with ease. Many crushers started learning to rock climb when they were young, training their bodies to grip and haul up rock faces and their minds to solve the puzzles posed by different climbing routes.

Indoor climbing walls help new climbers improve quickly and can also be great fun.

LEARN TO CLIMB

Rock climbing takes skill. Anyone wanting to try this exciting sport should start out in the safe and friendly environment of a climbing wall. Coaches here teach important safety skills as well as the basics about climbing. Most climbing walls also hire equipment at reasonable rates, which is a good option for beginners. When climbers are ready to take the next step and head outside, they can take a course with a qualified instructor to learn how to safely climb on real rock.

TOP ROPING

Top roping is what most people think of when they think of rock climbing. In top roping, a climber wears a harness that is attached to a rope by clips. The rope passes up through an anchor system at the top of the climb, and down to a belayer at the bottom. A belayer is a person who takes in slack rope while their partner climbs, so that if the climber loses their grip, they fall only a short distance.

GET FIT

Budding rock climbers need to be fit. Climbing rocks requires a strong core, good grip, and sturdy arms and shoulders. Climbers need powerful leg muscles because they use their legs to push themselves up, rather than rely on their arms to pull their body up the rock. Climbers also need to be flexible so they can stretch and reach their body around tricky patches of rock. So, before hitting the hills, climbers should hit the gym.

GIRL TALK

As well as being fun and a good way to keep fit, rock climbing and bouldering are great ways to make friends. Rock climbers usually work in pairs, with one person belaying while the other is climbing. Working together like this forges strong friendships.

Climbers often enjoy their sport with a climbing buddy.

No Man's Land

Some female climbers are not content to climb just for fun or for the challenge of competing against themselves. They want to break records and climb higher or harder than anyone else. These climbers tackle the toughest routes around the world.

TAKE IT TO THE LIMIT

Climbing routes are rated on a scale from 5.0 (easiest) to 5.15 (hardest) in what is called the Yosemite Decimal System. Climbs above 5.10 are for the best of the best. Bouldering has its own rating system, known as the V Scale, named for the bouldering pioneer John "Vermin" Sherman. It goes from V0 (easiest) to V17 (hardest). Very few people in the world have ever bouldered V16 and V17 routes.

GIRL TALK

Indoor climbing and competition-style climbing are very different from climbing on actual rocks. However, many climbers do both because they enjoy taking part in indoor competitions. In 2020, climbing will be an event in the Olympic Games for the first time, so some rock climbers are already training indoors in the hope of winning a medal.

Climbing athletes train indoors and outdoors to become the best they can be.

ASHIMA SHIRAISHI—MOVING MOUNTAINS

Ashima Shiraishi is one of the most accomplished female climbers in the world. While just a teenager, she became the first woman and the youngest person to complete a V15-rated boulder climb. At the 2017 International Federation of Sport Climbing (IFSC) Youth World Championships in Austria, she won three medals: gold in Bouldering and Sport, and a silver in Combined.

STARTING OUT

Ashima was born on April 3, 2001, in New York. She started climbing with her father at Rat Rock in New York City's Central Park when she was just six years old. At the age of 10, she became the youngest person to climb a V13, and in 2016, she achieved her V15-grade climb. Ashima has played a lead role in women's progress in the sport by breaking expectations of what women can do. She is also a spokesperson for sports gear-maker North Face's global initiative, Move Mountains, which is aimed at celebrating and promoting women in wild sports.

Japanese-American climber Ashima Shiraishi trains by climbing for an average of three to five hours a day, five days a week.

While outdoor climbing is her first love, Shiraishi now has her sights set on the Olympics, and is really excited that climbing has finally entered the frontier of a more mainstream sport.

There is no doubt about it—hunting is seen as one of the most macho outdoor sports of all. And yet, there is a new kind of hunter in the woods and she knows that in the world of hunting, it does not matter if the participant is a man or a woman. In the wild, only your skills matter.

Women looking for an exciting new challenge might consider the wild sport of hunting.

TRUE HUNTERS

People first hunted out of necessity. If they did not hunt for food, they would not have survived. Today, hunting is a sport. However, it is not just about shooting a gun or an arrow or wielding a knife to kill a wild animal. True hunters still take part in the sport to harvest their own food. They are responsible, ethical people who kill only the animals that they intend to eat and no more. They care about the environment in which they hunt and they do what they can to preserve and protect it.

TRACKING

A big part of hunting is tracking. To track animals, hunters study animal behaviors and habits. They learn to spot the differences between footprints left in dirt, droppings animals leave behind, and teeth marks or animal rub marks left on trees and other plants. Hunters also know how to sneak up on animals without being seen, heard, or smelled.

Hunters learn to walk through woods quietly, without stepping on every twig. They move slowly and stay behind cover of trees and brush as much as they can. They stay downwind of prey to keep their scent from blowing toward the animals. There are certain codes hunters follow. For example, they do not shoot an animal such as a deer if it has a baby. Without its mother, the baby deer would not survive.

Deer have eyes on the sides of their head so they can see predators creeping up on them. They also have a good sense of smell and excellent hearing.

GIRL TALK

All hunters must know and obey wildlife management laws that protect animal populations. Each year, they have to buy hunting licenses or tags. These give them permission to kill a limited number of a certain type of animal during a specified period of time or hunting season. Money from the sale of the licenses goes to the state for land and habitat conservation.

Male and female hunters face the same challenges. Animals do not run faster from a man than a woman.

Taking Aim

Hunters track an animal until they are close enough to shoot, or they hike until they find a good spot, such as a watering hole or river, where animals come to drink. Then they sit still, waiting patiently until an animal breaks into the clearing and enters their line of fire. Only then are they ready to take aim and shoot.

SHOOTING

Before anyone learns to shoot, they should learn about gun safety. They should know and understand the mechanics of how a gun works, how to load and unload it, how to check the gun chamber, and turn the safety on and off. They should know the correct way to carry a gun through wild areas such as woodland. Only then should they start to practice raising the gun to their shoulder, setting their sights on a target, and pulling the trigger.

Learning gun safety is an essential part of learning to shoot a gun.

FIELD DRESSING

When an animal has been shot and killed by a bullet or an arrow, hunters must find where it has fallen and act quickly to field dress it. Field dressing is the process of removing a dead animal's internal organs. This takes some getting used to, but it is an important way to preserve the animal's meat so that it can be eaten at home.

GET YOUR GUNS

Hunting equipment protects people against the elements but also helps them track and hunt. Hunters need clothes that are not only comfortable and keep them warm and dry, but that are also made from materials that do not make a noise when they move, because this can scare off wildlife. Jackets and pants with camouflage patterns help hunters blend in with the scenery and make it harder for prey to spot them.

GIRL TALK

Hunting is a dangerous sport if people wander into another hunter's shooting zone without realizing it, because they may be shot. As well as looking for prey, hunters must always be on the lookout for other hunters.

Some US states require hunters to wear a bright color called blaze orange. Deer and many other game animals cannot see this color, but other hunters can, so wearing blaze orange makes hunting safer.

Girls with Guns

There are many female hunters who not only enjoy their sport, but also do what they can to inspire other women to get outside to track, hunt, and shoot. Whether they are experts in archery or firearms, they strive to empower other women to break stereotypes and give hunting a try.

HUNTING BONUSES

Girls who hunt do not have to be super fit, but they do need to be fit enough to walk distances, climb through brush and up mountains, and drag large game with nothing but a rope. As well as providing hunters with exercise and fresh air, hunting also helps them develop discipline, patience, confidence, and endurance. It teaches people how to deal with disappointment and to move on and try again.

Hunting is good exercise. Even carrying a rifle and other equipment is a workout in itself.

RACHEL VANDEVOORT— QUEEN OF THE OUTDOORS

Rachel VandeVoort grew up hunting, fishing, and exploring northwest Montana with her father. Hunting was just part of family life because her father was not only a knife maker, but also a hunting, fishing, and rafting guide. Rachel killed her first deer when she was 12 years old and, as a youth, entered a lot of rifle competitions. One of her strongest memories is of her first elk hunt, after hiking 7 miles (11 km) into remote backcountry.

OUTDOORS FOR EVERYONE

Rachel is always outdoors—rafting, camping, fly-fishing, hunting, or skiing. She also spends a lot of time teaching others hunting and fishing skills, mentoring newcomers to the sports. In 2017, she became the first female director of a State Office of Outdoor Recreation in the country, working to promote outdoor recreation in Montana for all.

Successful hunters enjoy the challenge of tracking animals in all kinds of difficult weather.

GIRL TALK

Many female hunters say that one thing they love about the sport is the camaraderie and bonds they experience among fellow hunters. Many say that it is great to share the outdoors with people who value it as much as they do.

Chapter 4

Fly-Fishing

To the outside world, the sport of fly-fishing may look like a male-dominated activity, but there is a large number of female anglers who are combing the rivers and streams to find the best spot to enjoy their sport.

FISHING ON THE FLY

In fly-fishing, the name of the game is trying to outsmart, or trick, the fish. This involves dangling a lure, or artificial bait, in or on the surface of the water to attract a fish. The lure is typically a tiny model of an insect that mimics a fish's natural food. The fish swims up to take the fake fly and is caught on the hook, which is also attached to the end of the line. Then it is up to the angler to pull in the line quickly and efficiently, so the fish does not have a chance to wriggle free of the hook. The catch is then guided securely into a net.

Some people find fly-fishing a great way to be outdoors, be active, and also to have fun.

TAKE THE CHALLENGE

What makes fly-fishing tricky is the lightness of the lure. When fishing, anglers cast, or throw, their line over their head and into the water. A fishing line itself is very light, so the lure or bait attached to the end of the line is usually the heaviest part and the part that carries the lightweight line behind it when cast through the air. In fly-fishing, the lure or bait is also light, so it is much harder to cast the line far.

These are fly-fishing lures used for tempting and catching salmon.

GIRL TALK

When planning trips into the backcountry, be bear aware. In most situations, humans and bears coexist peacefully in the wild, but some anglers take bear spray as a first defense in case of an encounter. Bear spray contains a chemical that causes irritation in the bear's eyes, nose, and throat, to give people a chance to get away.

Most times a person encounters a bear, the bear will turn its tail and run.

Getting Hooked

Fly-fishing is one of the most difficult of all fishing techniques to master. But like most things that are difficult to learn, the rewards can be immensely satisfying. New anglers soon become hooked on the sport.

READING THE WATER

The first lesson anglers must learn is how to "read" the water. Fish live in different parts of a stream, river, or lake. If anglers do not learn where those places are, they end up spending most of their time fishing at spots where there are no fish. So, it is important to figure out where fish are most likely to be and how far a line and lure will drift to catch a fish.

Fly-fishing takes a lot of thought and a great knowledge of the river and fish feeding patterns.

LEARNING TO FLY-FISH

The key to fly-fishing success is correctly casting the line. To be able to do this well, beginners can watch some videos or take a lesson from an experienced angler. The idea is to grip the rod as if shaking someone's hand, then flick the rod backward and then forward quickly. This should throw the fly rod and the fly line so that they work together and the weight of the line carries the lure or bait out into the water.

STAYING HOOKED

Once hooked, a fish will try to escape. Fish can come off the hook if the hook is not sharp enough or if the angler lets the line go slack as the fish is pulled in and the fish is able to shake its head. Using a sharp, good-quality hook, setting it properly, and not letting the line slacken or go floppy when pulling in a catch should ensure fish stay hooked.

GIRL TALK

Getting to know which insects different fish like to eat and where those insects live means anglers can catch live flies and use those to lure their fish to their lines.

DRY FLY-FISHING

Dry fly-fishing is a technique in which the lure is an artificial fly that floats on the surface of the water and does not get wet. It is tricky to get the fly to land properly on the water in the right place, but it is great fun to see a fish such as a large trout rise up and nip on a fly floating on the surface.

Catching a Big One

Today, fly-fishing has seen a huge rise in female participants. While some fly-fishers are content to catch fish for food, others enjoy taking part in national and international fly-fishing competitions.

IN IT TO WIN IT

Fly-fishing competitions are often designed to test all of an angler's skills, and there are different rules and categories for the various events. Some have limits on the number of flies that can be used on a line or the length of a rod, for example. Points are awarded in different ways, too. Each fish caught may be worth a number of points, or fish are measured for length, or sometimes by weight. Anglers may compete as individuals or as part of a team. Dedicated fly-fishers battle it out for prizes, medals, and fame.

GIRL TALK

Fish caught at fly-fishing competitions are usually thrown back into the water so they can swim away after being caught and counted. Some fly-fishing sportspeople always catch and release, or let go, the fish that they catch.

Being photographed with a winning catch is a great way to remember a successful competition.

CASSIE SPURLING—FLY-FISHING WONDER

Cassie Spurling began fly-fishing when she was just five years old. Her father taught her how to fish in the mountains of North Georgia, where she still lives today. At first, she was very frustrated by how hard fly-fishing seemed when it came so easily to her father, but that spurred her on to want to cast as well as he did.

TEACHING OTHERS

Cassie has managed to make a career out of her passion for fly-fishing by becoming a guide in North Georgia. Her job has enabled her to improve her fly-fishing skills even more. She says: "I love sharing my passion with others and cherish the ability to teach the sport that has become such a huge part of my life. There is nothing like getting a client on their first fish and seeing the excitement and joy in their eyes."

Helping other women learn to love fly-fishing is one of Cassie's jobs as a guide in North Georgia.

Chapter 5

Caving

Just thinking about going underground can cause even the bravest to break out in a cold sweat. Yet those who venture below Earth's surface say that the wild sport of caving is an experience of nature unlike any other.

GETTING IN DEEP

It takes great courage to venture down into the underground world of dark and unknown tunnels and caves. Cavers may walk, climb, twist, squeeze, and crawl through passageways, scale rocky walls, or wade and swim through waist-high sections of water to reach caves. Deep in the darkness, the only light they have is the light that they bring with them. Yet, the rewards are immense when a tunnel opens out into a vast cave of sculpted rocks and delicate formations that are an awesome sight to behold.

Caving often involves crawling through tight spaces, climbing over rocks, and maneuvering between jagged rock formations.

CAVING DANGERS

Caving, like other sports in the wild, can be perfectly safe when done properly, but the sport does hold its dangers, and caving accidents and injuries do happen. Problems occur when cavers get lost in a cave, run out of light, become hypothermic, or slip and fall, sometimes down a crevice or hole in the rocks. Other dangers include falling rocks from unstable cave roofs and flooding of tunnels if rainstorms outside cause passes to fill with water suddenly.

CAVE DIVING

Cave diving is an extreme version of caving in which people swim in caves that are filled with deep water. They may hold their breath for short dives or take a tank of air so that they can stay underwater for longer. Not many people attempt cave diving, however, because it requires a lot of technical equipment and skill, and it is potentially very dangerous.

GIRL TALK

To avoid disaster, cavers must plan trips well. It is vital that they check weather forecasts if they are headed into a cave with streams. They must take all the equipment and supplies they think they might need, and let several people know about their caving plans. These should include exactly where they are going, who is going with them, and when they plan on returning home.

Cave diving is exciting but also potentially dangerous, so it is vital that divers know what they are doing and never go alone.

Daring the Darkness

Have you ever wondered what lies deep beneath the ground people walk on and the hills they climb? The best thing for beginners who wish to dare the darkness is to start out by taking a guided caving tour and lessons from an experienced caver. Unless cavers are tackling the deepest caves, most explorations can be done by crawling, wading, walking, and a little climbing.

Strap on a helmet! Caves are often wet and muddy, so cavers can slip and hit their head easily.

GETTING INTO GEAR

As well as a map of the cave route, if one is available, and a first aid kit for any cuts and bruises, there are some important pieces of equipment that all cavers need:

- Layers: Layers of clothing keep cavers warm, but they should choose fabrics that dry quickly when wet and will not rip easily when snagged on rocks.
- Lights: Cavers should wear a head-mounted lamp that straps onto the helmet, and carry two other lights, such as flashlights, glow sticks, or small light-emitting diode (LED) lights, and some extra bulbs and batteries.
- Knee and elbow pads: These provide protection when cavers are crawling.
- Gloves: Gloves protect hands from cuts and keep oils from cavers' hands from damaging delicate cave formations.
- Helmet: A caver's helmet should fit tightly and securely so it can protect their head if it is bumped on rocks or if rocks fall.

TEAMWORK

Caving is not a wild sport to tackle alone. Even experienced cavers go with at least one buddy and often in teams. They use spotting techniques to help each other over a difficult area, ensuring that everyone is safe. Cavers always stay together and keep the slowest caver in the front of the group, to reduce the risk of leaving anyone behind. Even in a relatively easy cave, caver teams and buddies stop frequently to check how everyone is doing.

Never go caving alone. A good group size of four to six people with an experienced guide is the safest way to go.

GIRL TALK

To protect the wild spaces they love to explore, cavers make it a general rule not to leave anything behind in a cave. That means wrappers, food waste, and even human waste. So, even though it might sound a bit disgusting, cavers always carry a plastic bottle to pee in, toilet paper, and a container or sealable bag to collect solid waste.

Sisters Who Squeeze

Women who choose to go caving may travel the world in their search for new adventures and increasingly difficult caverns. Those who are more experienced may travel many miles of tunnels and descend into the deepest, darkest caves, some as deep as the Empire State Building is tall, and sometimes into parts of caves never visited before.

GETTING SERIOUS

More serious cavers require additional equipment. If they are entering a deep, vertical cave where they will be descending several hundred feet, they will need climbing gear such as ropes, harnesses to attach them to the ropes, and gadgets called ascenders and descenders to help them get up and down those ropes quickly. As well as the equipment itself, these cavers need to know how to use it safely and properly.

Deep caving is a physically strenuous activity and requires a high level of fitness and strength as well as technical equipment.

GIRL TALK

A basic rule cavers follow is not to take any unnecessary risks. They should always look for the safest and easiest way to navigate the cave, not the fastest. Any injury, no matter how small, can be disastrous in a cave.

NIKKI GREEN—EXPEDITION CAVER

Nikki Green grew up in Frederick, Maryland, and became hooked on outdoor adventures in high school while on a training camp for the cross-country team in the Appalachian Mountains. She started caving at the University of Maryland with the Terrapin Trail Club.

Nikki has been preparing for and participating in cave expeditions around the world for years, and spends as much of her free time as she can exploring and surveying new caves and climbing rock, ice, and mountains.

TOO CLOSE

Nikki has had her share of close shaves, too. When one cave flooded after sudden rains above ground, some of Nikki's team got out but she and another caver had to sit and wait, not knowing if the tunnel would clear. Eventually, the water dropped enough for them to climb out, but this was a harsh reminder not to stay too long in a tunnel or cave again.

Cavers must remember to save enough energy to get back up again. However far they travel into a cave is as far as they have to travel out!

Chapter 6

Mad for Motocross

Motocross is a high-octane motorcycle sport that takes place on gravel, mud, or grassy tracks. It is a bit like cross-country racing on motorcycles. Although motocross is often seen as a rough and wild activity, it is a highly skilled, exciting sport that is enjoyed by women all over the world.

MOTOCROSS RACES

In a motocross race, riders compete on a course marked out over open and often rough, unlevel ground, covered with obstacles such as mounds of dirt. Motocross courses vary in distance but must be 1 to 3 miles (1.5 to 5 km) long in international competitions. To make the race more challenging and exciting, race routes include steep uphill and downhill sections, wet or muddy areas, jumps, and many left and right turns of varying difficulty.

Motocross is one of the most popular motorsports in the world.

HIT THE DIRT

Motocross races are also known as scrambles, for good reason. Riders not only have to speed along straighter sections, but they also scramble awkwardly up steep slopes or over rough ground. They shift their weight from side to side to whip around corners and maneuver their bikes while at full speed. They fly above many of the bumps and off dirt mounds, bravely holding onto their motorbike as the impact tries to throw them off.

The thrills and spills of motocross keep audiences on the edge of their seats.

TYPES OF MOTOCROSS

There are different types of motocross. Desert motocross racing, as the name suggests, involves racing over the sand dunes and uneven trails in the desert. In freestyle motocross, or FMX, events, motorcycle riders attempt to impress judges with jumps and stunts. Supercross is an indoor version of motocross that is run on artificial dirt tracks in large stadiums. Supercross is similar to motocross except supercross tracks are shorter and have more frequent and longer jumps.

GIRL TALK

Motocross is not without its risks. The chances are that riders will fall off their bike at some point and injure themselves. It all depends how fast and high they go and what tricks and jumps they try to do, but cuts, bruises, and broken bones are not uncommon.

Motocross riders defy gravity with their crazy turns and leaps.

Dainty Daredevils

It is great to ride motocross tracks just for fun, but women who tackle the jumps and bumps while racing against other riders say it gives them a different rush altogether. Motocross races are a thrill to watch and a huge buzz to take part in, but it takes time, dedication, and hard work to have the skill level required to compete.

GET UP TO SPEED

Before tackling any dirt tracks, motocross riders must learn to ride their motorcycle well. Then they start to scramble over dirt tracks, learning to handle their motorcycle on the uneven and moving sand, dirt, and mud routes. They can then gradually start to learn some jumps and tricks, beginning with the simplest ones first and gradually building up to higher jumps and stunts as their confidence and skills grow.

GIRL TALK

Motocross is probably the most physically demanding motorcycle sport of all. Riders must be super fit. They need strength and stamina to hold onto and control their motorcycle and make it to the checkered flag at the end of a grueling race.

Learning to ride motocross is great fun, but it helps if people already know how to ride a bike before they begin.

Case Study

TARAH GIEGER—MOTOCROSS MEDALIST

Tarah Gieger is a record-breaking motocross rider. In 2007, she became the first female racer ever to compete in the Motocross des Nations, an annual team motocross race nicknamed the "Olympics of Motocross." In 2008, she became the first female gold medalist ever in a moto event, winning the first women's supercross event at the X Games XIV, an annual extreme sports event run by broadcaster ESPN.

TOTAL DOMINATION

Tarah's parents moved from Puerto Rico to Florida before she was born, on September 18, 1985. Her parents owned a local surf store, so it is not surprising that she started out her sporting career surfing, but she switched to motorcycles when she was 10 years old. She never looked back and is now an international women's motocross star who says: "I won't be satisfied until I dominate women's motocross."

Motocross riders like Tarah fly through the jumps and the bumps of the racetrack.

ATV Motocross

Ready to go full-throttle? ATV motocross is extreme, fast-paced dirt-track racing on all-terrain vehicles, or ATVs. Riders slide around a racing track, taking tricky turns just inches apart, and spraying up huge clouds of dirt as they battle for position.

ATV motocross vehicles—or quad bikes—offer riders thrills and speed!

READY, SET, RACE!

ATVs are much like a motorcycle in that they are mostly ridden by one rider only and they are steered using handlebars. However, ATVs are both bigger and heavier, and they also have four wheels, which is why they are sometimes called quad bikes. ATVs are designed to be used off-road or on dirt roads, so their tires are large and there is a seat in the middle for riders to straddle. ATVs can still move fast, as they have big and powerful engines that enable them to reach speeds of 65 miles per hour (105 km/h) or more. ATV riders compete on the same tracks as motocross, or dirt bikes, often on the same day.

ATV ALTERNATIVES

ATV riders have a choice of sports. Motocross ATV racing takes place on a dirt circuit track, designed to have sharp corners and jumps of varying sizes. Cross-country races vary in length and are held in the countryside, usually in wooded areas or desert, and often include motocross sections. ATV freestyle involves an aerial display of tricks. Tricks are done for shows or are scored by judges in competitions. Some motocross and ATV tricks and stunts have some crazy names, such as the Superman. In this trick, a rider holds tight to the handlebars and lets their legs fly out behind them like the superhero Superman while in the middle of a jump.

GIRL TALK

The thrills and spills of ATV racing come with some serious safety risks. ATVs can be hard to control and unstable at high speeds. If they roll over or two ATVs crash into each other, injuries happen, sometimes even death. So, before getting on an ATV, riders should make sure they follow safety precautions and understand how to operate the vehicle safely.

In an ATV race, riders keep a close watch on riders coming up behind them and switch from left to right to prevent competitors overtaking them.

Quad Squad

The days of ATV racing being a guys-only game are over, and more and more women are outpacing the boys on their quad bikes. ATV riding requires a lot of skill, determination, and practice.

RACE TO WIN

Practice makes perfect—this motto is as true in ATV motocross as in any other sport. It is not enough to simply spend time riding on an ATV. Riders who want to compete should also spend a good amount of time on a practice track before they actually try to race. They should also take some time to work out with some running or swimming. Building up stamina using aerobic exercises like these will greatly increase a rider's chances of not tiring during a tightly fought race.

GIRL TALK

For safety's sake, riders should take a training course to learn how to drive an ATV safely, and use ATVs that are designed for their specific size and age. Riders should always wear a good-quality helmet and eye protection. In many states, it is against the law to ride without these.

Just because an ATV has four wheels does not mean it cannot roll over, so riders always wear safety equipment, including a helmet.

Case Study

SHELBY ANDERSON— FASTEST FEMALE

Shelby Anderson is not afraid to race ATV with the boys or girls. In 2018 she scored her first-ever professional victory when she won the utility terrain vehicle (UTV) World Championship Short Course Race, an event that was part of the Best in the Desert Series.

LOOKING TO THE FUTURE

Shelby lives in Riverside, California, and was introduced to racing at a very young age because her father and his family loved racing. She started racing go-karts at the age of five and her love of motorsports grew from there. When she was seven years old, she switched to ATV, and as her skill has grown, she has competed in national and world off-road championships. She is in full force in World Off Road Championship Series (WORCS) races, the biggest national off-road motorcycle racing series in the United States, and combines motocross with desert and off-road racing. So far Shelby has racked up more than 20 wins, and she has no plans for letting up. She says: "I'm excited to see where racing takes me in the future."

Shelby Anderson is challenging the view of UTV and ATV racing being for boys and proving that women are not only capable of surviving races but winning them.

Like Shelby, you need to be fearless to do well in UTV.

Becoming a Supergirl

Not so long ago, some girls and women may have been turned off the idea of sports in the wild because of their macho reputation, but today these awesome activities are available to everyone. There are more and more girls and women heading out into the wilderness to try a new challenge. What about you? Have you got what it takes to become a sporting supergirl?

GIRL POWER

Winning prizes and being first past the finish line in a race are not all it takes to make someone a supergirl. When a person devotes themselves to learning and becoming good at a new sport, such as fishing, hunting, riding motocross or ATVs, exploring deep caves, or climbing high rocks, they gain more than just new skills. They gain confidence, strength, fitness, and a determination to succeed in all walks of life, and these are the qualities that truly make a supergirl!

Learning to do a new activity well takes determination and dedication, but it sure feels good, too!

MAKE IT HAPPEN

Supergirls who want to compete in their sport, perhaps even at an international level, need to put in a lot of time and a lot of effort. To be able to practice for hours, you will have to give up other things to devote time to training. It may not be an easy ride, but it could be amazing fun.

CAREERS IN THE WILD

As well as doing sports in the wild for thrills and fresh air, or to compete and win prizes or fame, it is possible to forge a career from the activity you love. Some sporting supergirls share their experience and skill by becoming trainers or mentors, teaching others to become good at their sport. Others get jobs working for the companies that design or make sporting equipment. Or they work with organizations that stage championships and competitions or promote those events. Or they write features or blogs about the great women in wild sports to encourage other girls to join in, too!

GIRL TALK

No matter which wild sport you choose, put safety first. Wear the right equipment, learn the correct techniques, and when you are outdoors, never forget layers of warm clothes for colder days and sunscreen on hot ones. Sunlight can burn skin quickly when you are outdoors having fun, so take care.

As well as gaining skills, you may find some new friends when you take up a new wild sport.

Try It Out!

Find out just how great girls can be at all kinds of sports, then find your inner supergirl and try them out for yourself! The term "wild sport" covers a large number of different activities, so there is sure to be one that appeals to you.

Regardless of what you are into—whether it is caving, climbing, or motocross—there are plenty of places, people, and clubs around the United States that can help you learn about and enjoy sports in the wild.

HIKING

The American Hiking Society promotes hiking by inspiring and equipping people to get out on the trail: https://americanhiking.org

ROCK CLIMBING

To learn basic rock climbing skills, you could try an Outward Bound course. To find one in your area, go to: www.outwardbound.org/course-finder

The American Alpine Institute also offers courses in rock climbing: www.alpineinstitute.com/programs/courses/rock-climbing

HUNTING

There are rules, regulations, and very specific skills needed to hunt safely. Find an instructor or hunting education course via: www.ihea-usa.org/hunting-and-shooting/hunter-education/find-a-course

FLY-FISHING

The mission of Fly Fishing Team USA is to educate and train men and women in the sport of competitive fly-fishing. Find out more about the organization at: www.flyfishingteamusa.com

CAVING

Contact a local grotto (caving club) by going to www.caves.org and clicking the "Caving" menu, then "Find a Local Club."

MOTOCROSS

To find a beginner's course in motorcycle riding, try the Motorcycle Safety Foundation's Basic Rider Course. Find one near you at: www.msf-usa.org/brc.aspx

Find a dirt bike school at this website: http://www.dirtbikeschool.org

ATV RIDING

To find a proper ATV course, go to: https://www.arra-access.com/arra-toolbox/educational-opportunities

GIRL TALK

Once you know what sort of wild sport you want to learn, speak to a few different teachers, read some reviews, and maybe watch videos of the sport you want to try. Even if a class or course looks challenging, it is worth giving it a chance—you are there to learn a new skill, get in shape, and have fun!

Take aim and set your sights on a new wild sport if you have a spirit of adventure.

Glossary

aerobic exercise that makes people breathe hard and the blood pump through their veins faster as it carries oxygen to the muscles

camaraderie a feeling of friendliness toward people you work or share an experience with

camouflage colors and patterns that help someone to blend in with their surroundings

compass a device that has a dial and a magnetic needle that always points north

conservation the protection of nature

core the muscles within the torso, not the limbs

crevices narrow openings in a rock or wall

endurance the ability to keep doing something for a long time

ethical relating to beliefs about what is morally right and wrong

exhilaration a feeling of excitement

global positioning system (GPS) a navigation system that uses signals from satellites and math to determine an exact location

gun chamber the part of a gun into which a cartridge is inserted before being fired

habitat the natural home or environment of an animal, plant, or other living thing

harnessed secured or held in place using a set of straps and belts

hypothermic having a dangerously low body temperature

impact the force of one object hitting another

light-emitting diode (LED) a device that glows when electricity passes through it

lure a man-made bait, often shaped like a prey animal, used to attract fish

mentoring giving someone younger or less experienced help and advice

passes narrower areas

precautions things done beforehand to prevent harm or trouble

prey an animal that is hunted by other animals

quad a group of four

remote far away or difficult to reach

spotting watching another participant from the ground as they climb, to help them land safely if they fall

stamina physical or mental strength that allows people to continue doing something for a long time

stereotypes widely held but fixed and oversimplified images or ideas

terrain an area of land and its features

trekking pole a stick that helps people walk long distances

utility terrain vehicle (UTV) an off-road vehicle with room for cargo and an overhead bar for protection in case of rolling over

vertical standing or pointing straight up

For More Information

BOOKS

Abdo, Kenny. *ATVs* (Off Road Vehicles). North Mankato, MN: Abdo Zoom, 2018.

Murray, Laura K. *Cave Explorer* (Wild Jobs). Mankato, MN: Creative Paperbacks, 2018.

Oachs, Emily Rose. *Fly-Fishing* (The Outdoors). Mendota Heights, MN: Focus Readers, 2017.

Perritano, John. *Motocross Racing* (Intense Sports). Vero Beach, FL: Rourke Educational Media, 2018.

WEBSITES

Read more about motocross at:
www.americanmotorcyclist.com

Learn about ATV safety at:
https://kidshealth.org/en/teens/atv-safety.html

For tips on learning fly-fishing, try:
www.wikihow.com/Learn-Fly-Fishing

Discover 20 amazing places for rock climbing at:
https://wilderness.org/20-wild-places-outstanding-rock-climbs